JOURNEY OF A
U.S. ARMY SOLDIER
TO
GOD'S ARMY

CATALINO A. CARINO

WESTBOW
PRESS®
A DIVISION OF THOMAS NELSON
& ZONDERVAN

WestBow Press books may be ordered through booksellers or by contacting:

WestBow Press
A Division of Thomas Nelson & Zondervan
1663 Liberty Drive
Bloomington, IN 47403
www.westbowpress.com
844-714-3454

Scripture taken from the King James Version of the Bible.

ISBN: 978-1-6642-0467-6 (sc)
ISBN: 978-1-6642-0466-9 (e)

Print information available on the last page.

WestBow Press rev. date: 12/09/2020

Catalino Carino and his wife Cecilia

Carino family from left to right Allen,
Cecile, Lino, and Catherine

DEDICATION

I dedicate this book to my loving wife Cecilia and my two children, Catherine and Allen.

FOREWORD

As pastor of Faith Baptist Church in Canoga Park, California, I have had the great privilege and honor to be Lino and Cecilia Carino's pastor for the past four years. I have read Lino's book and there is absolutely no doubt that God has uniquely prepared both he and his wife for such an undertaking.

This is the story of a wonderful couple who on a daily basis exemplify great faith in their great God. Through a myriad of health trials that would silence many a voice, Mr. Carino has raised his up with great confidence and praise for the Lord.

Proverbs 13:20 states, "He that walketh with wise men shall be wise…" I encourage you to take this walk with Mr. Carino and am supremely confident that you will be better for it.

Tim Rasmussen

INTRODUCTION

"But now, O LORD, thou art our father; we are the clay, and thou our potter; and we all are the work of thy hand." [Isaiah 64:8 King James Version (KJV)]

The Word of God says that God formed us from the dust of the ground. We are all indeed just clay and God is our Master Potter. We are God's handiwork. He gifts us with good times but also allows hard times. We all rejoice when blessings come, but we need to also embrace the difficulties that come our way. They are part of God's molding and refining process. God uses them to fashion us into a vessel fit for His own use.

I wrote this book to show how God worked and saw me through hardships in my life. I want to show God's hand in my life and how He shaped me to become the person He wanted me to be. I want you to see God and His infinite goodness.

This book will first take you to a barrio nestled by the foot of the Caraballo mountain range in the Northern Philippines. It is where my family's story began. It will show you God's faithfulness in the many seasons of my life. My only desire in telling my story is to bring glory to God's name and to share the gospel so that others will come to the saving knowledge of the Lord Jesus Christ. I hope this book will be an encouragement to you.

HARDSHIPS IN LIFE

God has His own way of shaping people. The place and circumstances may be different, but God allows each one of us to go through difficult times. After going through such times, I have learned, that even in brokenness, we can glorify His name. It is in our weakest moments where we can really and deeply appreciate our strength in the Lord.

My mother Dionisia was born in Balauan, La Union. La Union is a province in the northern Philippines. It is by the sea and is serenely beautiful. She remembers it with a lot of sadness though. It was there where her father unexpectedly died. She was only seven years old at that time. My grandfather's sudden passing reminds me of what is in James 4:14 "Whereas ye know not what shall be on the morrow. For what is your life? It is even a vapour, that appeareth for a little time, and then vanisheth away." [James 4:14 KJV] Tomorrow is never promised.

As the eldest in the family, my mother took on the responsibility of helping her mom take care of her younger siblings. She had three brothers and a sister. Her youngest brother was not even one-year-old back then. Death just came and took her father away and that caused havoc to the rest of the family. It was a hard life for them, but they had to survive. Her dad, who was the loving bread winner of the family, was suddenly gone. "Who is going to take care of us now?" she sobbed. Her mother had no answer; she just cried. Even when they wanted to help, my grandmother's relatives were poor, and they had nothing to spare. Things got so bad that they were forced to move closer to my grandmother's relatives in San Quintin, Pangasinan. My mother loved to go to school but she was given this huge responsibility of taking care of her younger siblings and quit school to stay home.

What happened to my mother's family also happened to my father's family. My dad lost his father when he was 9 years old. The loss caused his mom to get sick and it affected her ability to take care of her four kids. My dad Alejo had no choice but to live with his Uncle Jose, who became like a father to him. Life in our province became difficult, and it behooved my dad's uncle to move to Manila and work as a security guard in a cigarette company. After a few years, he decided to work as a gate guard at the United States Embassy in the Philippines. This change in his life would be instrumental in a significant change in my family's future.

Both my grandmothers went through so much due to the early deaths of their husbands. Both of my parents were affected by their sufferings. After the deaths of their fathers, their futures have never been so uncertain. "Where will our next meal come from? Will I ever be able to continue going to school?" These thoughts were some of their concerns. They learned that they just had to keep moving and swim against the current of life to survive. They could not afford to go to school and were obligated to share the responsibility of taking care of their younger siblings. Neither one completed elementary education. They envied their friends passing by to go to school, but who would watch their younger siblings when their mothers were away to earn a living? No one but them.

My parents' childhood and teenage years were tough. They were forced to grow up and to take on responsibilities beyond their years.

WORLD WAR II

On December 8, 1941, when my parents were in their late teenage years, Japan started to invade the Philippines. They heard on the radio that the Japanese Imperial Army was coming to occupy their town and would capture and perhaps even kill them if they did not follow orders. Amid fear and chaos, the village elders banded together and created a local survival plan. They started digging and made bomb shelters in the woods. They experienced many false alarms of raids and bombings, but one day the real one came. Fighter planes flew overhead and bombarded their village with bombs and machine guns. They all ran hurriedly to the shelters for safety. They saw their houses and possessions burn to the ground. Many families lost their love ones that day but fortunately my dad, my mom, and their families survived.

Japan occupied the Philippines for over three years. Those three years were the worst years of their lives. They practically lived in the woods. They only went out in the open to gather food. But through all their difficulties, they found themselves falling for each other. They got married not long after that. They were only nineteen and eighteen years old. Life for the young newlyweds was not easy, to say the least. Survival was their main goal. They heard horror stories about those who were captured and tortured by the enemy. Those were scary times, but it just drew them closer to each other. The hard times helped shape my parents. They learned how to survive under the hardest circumstances. They knew how it was to be without, so they learned to prepare and save for the rainy days. From that point on, it became their lifestyle.

WORKING HARD

Many people blame their circumstances for their failures, but for my parents, dreams were borne out of adversity. They dared to dream, and they worked hard for those dreams. Most of all, when things got really hard, they did not quit. As farmers from the northern part of the Philippines, my parents knew how to cultivate the land, plant the seed, and nurture and water that which was planted. Most especially, they knew the feeling of joy and gladness in harvest time.

In the Philippines, farming and poverty usually come hand in hand. We were poor, but we lived a happy life. We were taught about hard work and resilience. My parents loved us and taught us good manners. We always had food on the table. Along with planting rice and growing our own vegetables, we worked hard to raise our own chickens, ducks, pigs, and goats for our meat. We only went to the public market to buy cooking oil, salt, and other essentials.

As a young boy, I would help out in the rice fields. I remember a particular instance when I helped my Dad water the rice paddies to prepare it for planting. I observed a colony of ants working hard to move the food they had put away to higher ground as the water rose. I learned that as tiny as they were, ants knew how to prepare ahead of time and worked hard day and night. In Proverbs 30:25, the Bible said, "The ants are a people not strong, yet they prepare their meat in the summer." [Proverbs 30:25 KJV]

A VIRTOUS WOMAN

My mother is a great example of a virtuous woman. I always think of my mother every time I read Proverbs 31. She was a faithful wife to my father and a loving mother to her children. My mother earned money from selling pigs and chickens that she raised herself. Sometimes, farming was tough because of drought or crops would be destroyed by a powerful typhoon. My mother always tried her best in the way she knew how.

　　My parents learned to always prepare for the rainy days. They worked hard and grabbed every opportunity just to be able to provide for our family. They wanted to give us a decent life, good education, and a brighter future. When my aunt could not buy back her property that she pawned to a Chinese businessman in town, my parents redeemed and paid for it. That was how they finally had farmland they could call their own. And after a few more years, they bought more land. They sacrificed and saved just to send their eight children to school, where all of them did well. In their small farming village, which was about four kilometers from town, everyone had to walk to and back from school. Very few families sent their children to high school. Many parents had the mindset that once their children could read, write, and know simple arithmetic, there was no more reason to further their education. But my dad's Uncle Jose, who was now working as a gate guard for the US Embassy, advised my parents to do everything in their power to send their children to college. My Great Uncle Jose shared his vision with my parents and encouraged my dad to allow us to further our education. This would haul us out of poverty from the poor farming village.

NOT AGAIN

One day, my dad was planting rice seedlings for his farm. They were installing barbed wire fence around the seedlings when lightning hit the tree where they attached the barbed wire. My father and his helper were stunned by the powerful electrical shock. The lightning was so strong that it knocked them unconscious and they fell flat on the ground. No one saw them lying there while rain poured vigorously, flooding the ground. No one knew how long they were lying there unconscious. Somehow his helper regained his consciousness and was able to stand up. He moved my dad's unconscious body and laid his head higher than the accumulating rainwater. He hurriedly ran home and called for help. My mom heard the grave news and she just sobbed "not again." She lost her dad when she was only seven years old, now this depressing news. She refused to accept that she could lose her husband early in their marriage. Men from the neighborhood ran to get my dad. After checking him out, all of them pronounced him dead. He was not breathing and not responding. In those days in a remote village, no one knew CPR; if one was not breathing, he was basically dead. The men carried my dad home by putting his body in a makeshift stretcher made of a blanket tied to bamboo poles. This makeshift stretcher bounced up and down while they were carrying my dad to bring him home. My mother saw them approaching and saw the blanket like a body bag; she sobbed even more. She cried out to God and fervently asked for divine intervention. She was not a Christian then, but she believed there is God. When they arrived in front of her, they opened the blanket and my dad still dazed, miraculously greeted my mom. He asked her: "Where am I and what happened?" I believe that the bouncing helped revive him. My mom was incredibly grateful that dad was okay.

My parents went through another trial when a bull water buffalo gored my dad with its horn and injured him severely. It caused a large wound that required him to be hospitalized for a few weeks. Of course, he was not able to work during that time. No work and no income meant little food on the table; there was no health insurance; there was no sick leave nor paid time off. This trial wiped out my parents' savings. They had to get a loan to pay for hospital bills. This pushed them in deeper debt. My dad consoled my mom and said, "The good thing is, I am alive, and we can start all over again." With teary eyes, my mom just nodded and agreed "Yes, we still have each other." Indeed, despite their misfortunes, they did not stay low-spirited. They got up and moved forward.

MY PARENTS' VISION

My parents believed that for their children to have a better future and get out of poverty, education is a must. They made a pledge with each other to do everything in their capacity to send us all to college and get degrees. My parents had a good plan. Their plan was to send their older children to college until they graduate. In turn, they would then start working to help with the college expenses of the younger ones. It was a perfect plan, so they thought. Without it, their resources would be exhausted, and the younger ones would have no chance to attend college.

My eldest brother's dream was to become a police officer. He took up Criminology in college. When he was in his junior year, my parents ran out of money to support his schooling, so he joined the Philippine Army. While in boot camp, he was involved in a fistfight with another trainee. With his self-defense skills gained from his criminology classes, he gave the other trainee a whipping. The other trainee's friends planned to retaliate that night. They intended to inflict excessive bodily harm on my brother and perhaps even kill him. One of my brother's friends tipped him off about the plot and he escaped before it happened. In the darkness of night, he traveled by foot through thick forest, hills, and rivers until dawn. A traveling farmer picked him up and brought him to a nearby town where he took the bus to our great uncle's house in Manila. While looking for a job, he was advised by our Great Uncle Jose to take the United States Navy entrance exam. My brother prepared for this exam for months. The day before the exam, my dad accompanied him on a ten-hour bus ride to Sangley Point Naval Station in Cavite. The exam started at 6:00 a.m. My father waited outside the gate praying. At 9:00 a.m., almost half of the examinees were out. My dad asked around "Why are they already out, where is my son?" He was told that those examinees coming out early did not pass the entrance exam. The news gave my Dad hope. He continued to pray. He was told that "If your son is not out by 11:00 a.m., it means he passed." It was indeed true. My brother finally came out at around 11:20 a.m. with a big smile on his face. He told my dad that he passed. My parents' hard work and sacrifices paid off. They celebrated and ate in a good restaurant. My brother was incredibly surprised; he told my dad "I thought you did not have any more money." My dad said, "This money would only be spent if you passed the exam."

My oldest brother left for the US Navy boot camp in 1969. With his salary, he started sending my parents money for the college expenses for the younger siblings. College was expensive and three of my siblings were in college at the same time. My parents had no choice but to pawn their farmland. They were determined that they would do everything to send their children to college. It broke their hearts to pawn their hard-earned farmland, but they did not have a choice. To help the family out, one of my aunts was kind enough and offered to pay for one of my brother's school expenses.

INSPIRING SACRIFICE

My parents made sacrifices for us. They almost lost all their farmlands for my siblings' college expenses. I remember when they would come home from college to get their personal allowance and funds for their tuition fees. When my parents did not have any money on hand, they would go to the town and pawn their farmland so my siblings could pay for their school expenses. It was a great sacrifice for them. Their plan for the older ones to finish college and start working to help the younger ones did not work out well though. Even when the older siblings finished their degrees and started working, their salaries were not even enough for themselves, let alone to spare money to help. People from other parts of the world may not understand this. But in the Filipino culture, this practice is not uncommon. The older brother or sister would be sent to college with the hope that when he or she is done and has a job, they would help the parents to shoulder the younger siblings' education expenses. I am the sixth child in our family. This plan did not work out for me.

When it was my time to attend college, I witnessed my parents' difficulties so I told them that I would not let them go deeper into debt to pay for my college education. I yielded and did not demand for them to send me to college too. I decided to work and just wait. I sacrificed my dreams and worked in the farm, and later, as a security guard in a gold mining company in Baguio City.

GOOD WORK ETHIC

My dream of being a sailor in the US Navy was born while working in the rice fields. God undoubtedly was already preparing me by the way my father trained and instilled discipline in me. At a young age, I was already working for my family in my parents' small farm. I got up at 5:30 a.m. and I would start working by feeding the chickens, taking care of the goats and cows, and did any other chores that needed to be done. My siblings and I did that before starting school at 7 a.m. I walked to school in the morning, would be back home at lunch time, and prepared to get back to school again until five in the afternoon. That was my daily routine.

From our small farm, my dreams to be in the US military seemed farfetched. I believe though that it was God who placed that dream in my heart. Our home was close to Clark Air Base, a US military base in the Philippines back then. Every day, I would hear the roar of the fighter jets and US Navy airplanes as they flew over my head when I was working in the rice fields. I remember looking up at the sky and I telling myself that one day I would be a member of the US Navy. I really wanted to be a sailor but with the advice of my eldest brother, I ended up joining the United States

Army. He said that sailors spend too much time away and it takes a toll on their families.

Our town was small, and people knew everybody. I remember seeing how families of US Navy personnel seemed way better off than farmers' families. I was even more determined to make a better life for me and my family. Back then, Filipinos were able to join the US Navy straight from the Philippines due to the joint agreement of the Philippines and the US government after World War II. That agreement allowed the US Navy to recruit directly from the Philippines. My eldest brother took that opportunity and was able to join the US Navy in 1969. Unfortunately, the agreement ended in 1992.

Hard work was engrained in me by my parents. I remember my dad would always tell me to make good use of my time. He would tell me to be keen and work hard. I was taught how to be resourceful too. I had to learn to fish so we would have something for dinner. There were rivers and small ponds around the area, so my father would sometimes take me there to fish. My father taught me all kinds of fishing techniques. He taught me how to catch crabs from the rice fields. Some people may not understand this because they have the mindset that crabs can only be found in the ocean. In the Philippines, we have rice field crabs. We fished at nighttime too. Early in the morning, we would pass by the brook and fetch the fishes that have been trapped in our fishnets.

We were all busy helping and doing our share for our family. We also had to tend our own vegetable garden and the fruit trees in our yard. Although we were poor, we never went hungry. Diligence can certainly make a big difference in life. Our hardships strengthened our bond as a family because we learned to work together.

When God created Adam and Eve, He provided for their needs. But idleness was never encouraged. The Lord made them work with their hands. "And the LORD God took the man, and put him into the Garden of Eden to dress it and to keep it." [Genesis 2:15 KJV]

TEENAGE YEARS

In 1973, after completing my elementary education, I went to the town high school. I came from the small village, a farm boy, and dark skinned. I did not have a sense of belonging. I really wanted to prove to myself and to the people around me that we, the village children, were just as capable as the children in the city. It made me work harder to compete with the other students. During my freshman year, I did so well that I made it to the top 10 in my class. I did not do as well during the succeeding years as I tried to seek acceptance from my peers rather than excel in academics. My parents continued to encourage me to keep going, to study hard, and finish my studies. Thanks to them, despite the challenges that I went through, my desire to do well was still there. I believe that although I was not a Christian at the time, I already had God's hand on me.

What I thought would be an inspiration to me when I had a teenage crush on this girl, turned out to be a nightmare. She was unkind and discriminated me because I was a poor farm boy from the barrio. The wound it inflicted on me was deep and followed me into adulthood. However, it motivated me to prove myself and work harder to succeed in life so that I would not be discriminated any longer. But when I got saved and got to know my Lord and Savior, the Lord gave me a different mindset. I realized that all blessings in life could only come from God.

I really wanted to attend college too, but my parents' hands were tied. Three college students were just too much for them to support. My parents could not afford to send me to college when it was my time to go. While waiting for my immigration petition, I decided to go to a training camp to be a security guard for a mining company. I had to go to boot camp for 2 months at Saint Louis University and Camp Dangwa, La Trinidad, Benguet. The training was intensive, but I learned a lot, especially how to do things on my own. It was different from my life in the province. Later, the mining company purchased a body scanner from the USA. It gave me a sense of pride that I was the one who controlled and operated the machine.

While working in Antamok Mines, I had my worst fist fight when I had a conflict with my fellow guard. It all started from joking and foolish talk. The other guy was suddenly enraged and punched me on my mouth. I was caught by surprise, and I was wondering what I have done to make him mad. We were drinking and he probably was already intoxicated at that point. I fought back and during the fight, company property was damaged. We were picked up by the Security Police Officer and taken to the company's security headquarters. During the investigation at the office, the others were insisting that it was my fault and that it was I who started the squabble. I was so furious, but my pleas and explanations were not heard. They favored the other guy who was the driver of the Chief of the Security Forces. They discharged me without any further opportunity to appeal. The discharge note may not be very encouraging at that time. But after more than a year as I picked up the pieces, I realized that God's hands were on me. I later heard the news that as my former coworkers were going to work one afternoon, the vehicle they were riding on went off a cliff. Only two survived in that accident. If I was still there, I might be one of the casualties. God must have spared my life for a reason.

I went back home to the village and back to farming. This time my mom and dad already moved to the US. Some of my siblings were still in college. I was out of school and out of a job. However, my dad had asked me to take care of the farm while I was waiting for my immigration papers to go to the US. It was an honor to take care of his hard-earned possession. While I enjoyed farming and doing it for my dad, I wished I were going to college like my siblings and my friends.

LEAVING THE BARRIO

The time came for my family to immigrate to the United States. First, my mother immigrated to San Diego, California in 1979. In 1980, my father joined her. My two older siblings and I followed in 1982, and in 1983, the rest of my siblings came except my oldest sister who was married at that time. We left the life we had in the Philippines behind and now live in the United States of America. Our adoptive country gave us so much promise and opportunities that we otherwise would not have.

I knew that being in the US military was where God was leading me. I worked hard to fulfil its requirements to get enlisted. It was in October of 1983 when I joined the Army. I tried to overcome all the challenges at the Army Basic Training Camp so I could fulfill my dream. It was a make it or break it situation for me. The difficulties in the training camp seemed to be nothing. I knew it was part of the process of making my dream come true. I had to get used to the cold weather and the three feet of snow. The funny part was I could not really understand my drill sergeant's southern accent. I spoke Ilokano and Tagalog and learned English only in school, but conversational English was still a challenge for me. I somehow got by, through imitating my fellow trainees. I only began to understand my drill sergeant after two weeks. It was only by the grace of God that I successfully completed the Army Basic Training. After that, I was sent for further schooling in Advanced Individual Training to learn my assigned military occupational specialty.

MARRIAGE AND FAMILY

[Proverbs 31:10 KJV] 10 Who can find a virtuous woman? for her price [is] far above rubies.

[Proverbs 18:22 KJV] 22 [Whoso] findeth a wife findeth a good [thing], and obtaineth favour of the LORD.

In March 1984, I was assigned to my first duty station in Fort Benning, Georgia. At the time, Fort Benning was the largest Army Base in the US, spanning fifty square miles. It was where I spent my early days as a soldier. It was where my wife and I had our first home. Back in 1982, I met my wife Cecile, and we became friends. She was introduced to me by my brother and sister-in-law. She was in the Student Exchange Program and they happened to meet her at her foster parent's home in San Diego. Cecile went back to the Philippines to finish her studies. I had the opportunity to meet her before I departed for the US. When I first saw her, in my mind and in my heart, I knew she was the woman that I was going to marry someday.

Cecile's parents believed in traditional values. They protected her from heartaches that would have come from wrong relationships. Because she felt nurtured and loved, she concentrated on her studies and put everything else on the back burner. I wrote her for two years. There were no social media back then.

Cecile traveled back to the US in 1984. The trip was a graduation gift from her parents. I heard that Cecile was in California. I called her often and we talked about everything. I realized my days were brighter and I was happier after talking to her. From Fort Benning, Georgia, I traveled to California just to see her. Since I came from afar and since she was friends with my brother and his wife, she agreed to go out with me. During the early days of our getting to know each other, she frankly told me that there was no immediate attraction, but she liked my personality. As we got to know each other better, feelings developed. The rest, as they say, is history. We got married in Los Angeles not long after that. I went back to Georgia and she followed me there after sorting out things and doing paperwork in California.

When she was in college, she was courted by many suitors, but she never went out with any of them. I honestly believe that God meant her for me. I always told her that she was the one made just for me; she smiles at me every time I mention that.

After we got married, we settled down in a military housing in Fort Benning. The following year, our daughter Catherine was born in the Martin Army Hospital. I could honestly say that God has been good to me.

GERMANY ASSIGNMENT

After my military assignment in Fort Benning, Georgia, I received assignment orders to go to Karlsruhe, Germany for a three-year military tour. We were so excited. I bragged to my wife that I was fulfilling my promise when I married her that I will take her around the world. I never imagined in my life that I would be working in Germany and had the opportunity to hop in a car on weekends and drive to other European countries. Switzerland, Austria, Italy, Netherlands, Belgium, France, and Luxembourg were just some of the countries we had the privilege to visit without spending thousands of dollars. We just hopped in a car and went. It was a dream come true for us. It was certainly a blessing from the Lord that I took for granted then. But looking back, now that I am a Christian, I thank God for the once in a lifetime chance to see the many beautiful sites in Europe.

It was in Karlsruhe, Germany where our son, Allen was born. My wife was having labor pains at the delivery room in a local German hospital at the same time the Berlin Wall was being toppled down. It was really a very memorable time for us. The Berlin Wall was falling when the German nurse handed me my son, Allen. President

Ronald Reagan persuaded President Gorbachev, and a great event happened; communism in that part of the world was finally over. When my son was released from the hospital, I was surprised when they handed me a birth certificate written in Deutsche.

THE REWARD OF DILIGENCE

The Bible says that the good Lord rewards hard work:

Proverbs 14:23 "23 In all labour there is profit: but the talk of the lips tendeth only to penury." [Proverbs 14:23 KJV]

Proverbs 12:11 "11 He that tilleth his land shall be satisfied with bread: but he that followeth vain persons is void of understanding." [Proverbs 12:11 KJV]

After Germany, we moved to Texas in 1990. I believe we were led by God there to further our education. Possessing a bachelor's degree from the University of the Philippines, my wife had the opportunity of studying for and acquiring the national math teaching certification. I also started pursuing my dream of earning my college degree. Remember, I did not get a chance to go to college in the Philippines. Though I had a career in the military, I did not totally abandon my dream of earning my college degree. Being a full-time soldier, husband, father, and a student all at the same time was extremely difficult. But I believed that if I put my priorities right, one day I would achieve my goal. In 2001, after many years of night and weekend classes, I finally earned my bachelor's degree in Computer Science. I gave a copy of my diploma to my parents and they shed many happy tears; they remembered that I was the one who yielded and took care of their farm while my siblings attended college.

We moved to Hawaii from Texas where my wife had the opportunity to work as a teacher. She taught high school math in Campbell High School in Ewa Beach and we lived nearby.

THE CONVERSION

For years, my mother-in-law has been encouraging us to visit a bible believing church. The answer to her prayers came one day. We were new to Hawaii and we did not know many people. Someone knocked on our door. It was an older lady who lived three doors down from us. She introduced herself and invited us to visit her church. We were excited to visit the following Sunday. The gospel was then shared and was explained to us for the very first time. We understood that Jesus died on the cross for our sins. He was buried and rose again the third day according to the Scriptures. We believed in what the Word of God said. We repented of our sins and accepted the Lord Jesus Christ as our Savior and Lord. It was the single most important decision that we made. It changed the direction of our lives. It also changed the eternal destination of our souls. My wife and I both got saved in October 1993. The salvation that we received in the Lord Jesus Christ is truly undeserved. It is the gift of God. The Word of God pierced our hearts and we have never been the same since.

These verses speak of our depravity as sinners, and God's redeeming love. They can help one understand God's free gift of salvation:

1. We are all sinners.
   a. [Romans 3:10 KJV] "10 As it is written, There is none righteous, no, not one;"
   b. [Romans 3:23 KJV] "23 For all have sinned, and come short of the glory of God;"

2. Death is the penalty of our sins.
   a. [Romans 6:23a KJV] "23 For the wages of sin is death…"

3. Christ died for us.
   a. [Romans 5:8 KJV] "8 But God commendeth his love toward us, in that, while we were yet sinners, Christ died for us;"
   b. [2 Peter 3:9 KJV] "The Lord is not slack concerning his promise, as some men count slackness; but is longsuffering to us-ward, not willing that any should perish, but that all should come to repentance."

4. God loves us so much and He willingly gave His only begotten Son. Jesus is the only way.
   a. [John 3:16 KJV] "16 For God so loved the world, that he gave his only begotten Son, that whosoever believeth in him should not perish, but have everlasting life;"
   b. [Acts 4:12 KJV] "12 Neither is there salvation in any other: for there is none other name under heaven given among men, whereby we must be saved;"

    c.   [John 14:6 KJV] "6 Jesus saith unto him, I am the way, the truth, and the life: no man cometh unto the Father, but by me."

5.   Salvation is a gift from God. We cannot earn it by good works.
    a.   [Romans 6:23b KJV] "...but the gift of God is eternal life through Jesus Christ our Lord;"
    b.   [Ephesians 2:8-9 KJV] "8 For by grace are ye saved through faith; and that not of yourselves: it is the gift of God: 9 Not of works, lest any man should boast."

6.   Confess and believe that Jesus is Lord.
    a.   [Romans 10:9-10 KJV] "9 That if thou shalt confess with thy mouth the Lord Jesus, and shalt believe in thine heart that God hath raised him from the dead, thou shalt be saved. 10 For with the heart man believeth unto righteousness; and with the mouth confession is made unto salvation;"

7.   Ask the Lord to save you.
    a.   [Romans 10:13 KJV] "13 For whosoever shall call upon the namc of the Lord shall be saved;"

It was because of His amazing grace that our Lord saved us, and He began to work in our hearts. We were no longer our own. We have been bought with a price, the blood of our Lord Jesus Christ. We belong to our Savior and we sought to please Him. This did not make us perfect people, just loved and forgiven. We felt humbled that Jesus, God's own Son would die for us knowing full well that we have failed Him countless of times. Oh, what a loving Saviour!

Not long after we made a profession of faith, an opportunity was offered to us when the pastor found out that my wife was a teacher. We started teaching Sunday school class for Juniors. It was such a blessing to be able to teach young children about Jesus. After our conversion, we dedicated our lives in the service of our King.

CALL OF DUTY

Being a computer analyst in the Army, we moved often from one station to another. It was hard for all of us. Every time we moved, there were adjustments to be made. We had to move all our household goods and find us a new home; may it be an apartment or military housing. Each time, we had to leave all the friends we made behind. As our children grew older, the process became harder. I had to adjust to a new work environment as well. Each move was not easy but that was what I signed up for in the Army. Knowing that God was with us wherever we went made us rest in the Lord and look forward to each move with joyful expectation.

After Georgia, Germany, Texas, and Hawaii, I was assigned to the Pentagon at the Defense Intelligence Agency (DIA) to manage the security clearance database of DIA personnel. I handled top secret information and my job required that my wife get her US Citizenship immediately. I felt honored that the US government gave that opportunity to an immigrant like me. The boy who grew up in a poverty-stricken village in the Philippines was privileged to work in the Pentagon handling sensitive classified information. Truly this country is the land of endless opportunities.

I also have short tours of duty while serving in the US

Army. I was sent to England to support the Kosovo conflict. I was sent to Bangkok, Thailand to support the Cobra Gold Military Exercise. I was sent to Manila, Philippines to support the Balikatan, a joint exercise between American forces and the Philippine Military. During unaccompanied tours of duty, it was hard for military spouses to be alone and take on all the responsibilities at home. Leaving my wife to take care of our young children was hard for her but that was the price we had to pay as a military family. As a soldier, I did what my Commander-in-Chief told me to do. This reminds me of when Jesus asked the apostles to follow Him and made them "fishers of men" Matthew 4:19 KJV. The apostles obeyed and left everything behind and followed Him.

PROMOTION IS
FROM THE LORD

In 1995, we were re-assigned to Hawaii for another important mission. It was a great blessing for me because I was promoted to Master Sergeant which is the second highest rank for Army Noncommissioned Officers. While in Hawaii we attended Ohana Baptist Church where we would worship, serve the Lord, grow in grace and in the knowledge of the Lord Jesus Christ. My wife and I were also privileged to be a part of the children's ministry called "Patch the Pirate" in our church. We realized that the most important thing in life is to be in the center of God's will. We need to be in the place where God wants us to be, doing what He wants us to do in the service for His kingdom.

From 2002 to 2007, my last military assignment was in Yokota Airbase, the headquarters of US Forces Japan. We found a church immediately when we arrived. The church was very mission minded and the pastor was deeply passionate about sharing the gospel to the lost. Again, we were blessed to be involved in the ministry of Yokota Baptist Church. While there, my wife taught Sunday school and I served as the church's treasurer and deacon. I also had many opportunities to preach when my pastor was in furlough in the US. During that time, I had no idea that God was already molding me to be a missionary evangelist. I also learned that the Christian life is about self-denial and service for God and others. My family and I did not get to see much of Japan because of my twelve-hour workdays and my church responsibilities. I have no regrets though. For me, first and foremost, I wanted to serve God, then my family, and my country.

GOD'S CALLING

The Lord's calling is sure, and He may call us anytime, anywhere, and to any ministry that we may think we are not equipped for. In 2004, God did something that I never expected. He called me in the ministry to do missions in the Philippines. We were actively serving in our church then and going back to the land of our birth would be a big adjustment for me and my family. But it was crystal clear for me when the Lord spoke to my heart and called me to be an evangelist. It was in Japan where God spoke to me when Pastor Warren Webster was preaching during our missions' conference. The Holy Spirit started speaking to my heart. I was also inspired by how much my pastor loved God and the ministry. He dedicated his whole life to the Lord. One day he told me that God called him to Japan to do ministry and that he obeyed God's calling even if it was not easy. He promised the Lord that he would stay in Japan and preach until the Lord calls him home. He was in his late 60's when I heard him say those words and they left a mark on me. My pastor left America, his children, and his grandchildren to heed a higher calling. I salute the boldness, the dedication, and the love that my pastor had for the Lord. After a few years, he went home with the Lord. He died while serving the Lord in Japan.

II TIMOTHY 2:3-4

2 Timothy 2:3-4 "3 Thou therefore endure hardness, as a good soldier of Jesus Christ. 4 No man that warreth entangleth himself with the affairs of this life; that he may please him who hath chosen him to be a soldier." [2Timothy 2:3-4 KJV]

I was reminded by the Lord that my concentration as His soldier must be on Him. It should be in Him and for Him. I could only do that if I become a true soldier of God, fighting the battle in His field. The Lord clearly laid it in my heart. If I disobey Him, I surely will have to pay for the price of my disobedience. I would rather pay the price in obedience to God and His calling. People seldom see soldiers cry but I did cry when I surrendered my life to God to be in the ministry. It may not be easy for us to follow God because we would be stepping into the unknown, but God knows what is out there. He has a plan for you and me. It may be a tough decision, but tough becomes tougher because we often do not trust the Lord and whatever plan He has for our lives.

I believe when the Lord called me that He would also equip me. He molded me, prepared the field and the people that I would work with to help spread the gospel of our dear Lord Jesus Christ. Our pastor was so happy when I told him that God called me to be a missionary evangelist. However, it was a big surprise for my wife. My wife was born a planner; she does not like surprises. Worries started to creep in into my wife's heart like many of those who were called by God. Remember that it may look like a big move for us, but not with God. Later, the Lord gave my wife the peace and assurance that she needed as it became clear to her that God called us to minister in the Philippines. I thank the Lord for my wife who was and is incredibly supportive to the call of God. We had to learn to trust the Lord and believe in His promise that He will be with us and He will not forsake us. I thank the Lord for our pastor who mentored us and helped us grow. The Lord used him to disciple us and train us for the ministry.

In 2004, we went to visit churches in the province of Bulacan, where my wife is from. We met several pastors who were in a Pastors and Workers' Conference as they shared their work and ministries. They were all excited to partner with us. It was such an encouragement for us to have met people in the ministry faithfully serving the Lord. Although God had already given us the confirmation of my calling in His Word, He reinforced it with this trip by showing me that the harvest is truly plenteous, but the laborers are few.

THE SACRIFICE WE HAD TO MAKE

To answer God's call in our lives, we would have to leave our children and the comforts of America. That meant trusting that God would be the one to look after and guide our children, who were young adults when we first started in the ministry. There were many other concerns, but we have seen God move. He was the one who paved the way, and He provided every need. He is indeed faithful! As for leaving the comforts that America has to offer, we had some adjustments to make. We have grown accustomed to the way of life here, but God prepared us a long time before He called us. We were both born and raised in the Philippines. Even after more than 30 years in our adoptive country, the Philippines is still the land of our birth. Anticipating the changes that come with every move is not easy, but we just had to embrace whatever challenges we had to face. Whatever sacrifices we had to make could not be compared to what our Lord Jesus did for us on the cross of Calvary. Jesus left the splendor of heaven. He was born, suffered, and died because He loves you and me.

RESPONSE TO GOD'S CALLING

Our response to God's calling depends on our attitude toward God and His work. In my case, my pastor at that time was preaching about missions and Lord convicted me at that moment. The Holy Spirit moved me to surrender my life for missions. I came forward and gave my life to God. I was compelled to reach out to the lost souls and share the saving gospel of the Lord Jesus Christ. I also felt the goodness of God and saw Him work in the heart of my wife. My wife's support and her obedience to the call of God was such a blessing to me. I appreciate her submission to the Lord and to me as her husband. My wife's surrendered heart towards the call of God despite the unknown certainly helped us in the transition. There were adjustments that we would have to make because of the differences in lifestyle and culture. Hence, we asked God for His guidance and His wisdom.

Our pastor was so generous of his time and knowledge of the Bible. Sharing it to us and other preacher boys who also went through discipleship and leadership training with me. We committed everything to God because we felt unprepared and a little fearful. We did not know exactly what to do and where to go in the Philippines. We sought the Lord's will and unbeknownst to us the Lord had already prepared the hearts of a couple of pastors. God was putting everything in place for us.

The Lord also prepared our children's hearts as evidenced by their submission and support to our calling. We did not need to step ahead of God. God knew and knows what is best. He had a plan and He prepared everything. The only concern our children had was that we would have to live away from them when we leave for the Philippines. They knew it was and still is God's calling for us; they also had to sacrifice and obey. I told them that God's presence and protection would be with us.

Serving the Lord should not be a burden but a blessing to us who follow His call. Our pastor taught the church to be mission minded, and it became the heart of the church. When God called me, I understood why evangelism and world missions are important. I also knew that God was calling me to the country that gave birth to me, the Philippines. It was in 2007 when I finally retired from the Army. In February of that year, my next military assignment was coming up. I knew, that if I did not retire, the potential of me going to war in Iraq at that time was eminent. Thus, the Lord guided me to retire from military duty so I could be in the ministry. Though my calling was clear to me, I felt inadequate. I felt I needed to prepare myself for this new journey. When I was in the US Army, I learned that a soldier must always be prepared. We are soldiers for Christ and therefore, we should prepare as such. We went back to the US to attend Bible Institute in California. While studying

Biblical Theology, I worked as a federal civilian employee in US Naval Base Ventura County.

After military service, my wife and I enlisted to become soldiers of God. Our work should be pleasing to Him. I needed to learn more about the Lord and His Word. My wife knew that she was included to my calling as my teammate, so she attended some classes too. Nobody goes to battle without the proper training.

2 Timothy 2:15 said "Study to shew thyself approved unto God, a workman that needeth not to be ashamed, rightly dividing the word of truth" [2 Timothy 2:15 KJV].

God wanted us to study and always be ready to give an answer.

1 Peter 3:15 "But sanctify the Lord God in your hearts: and be ready always to give an answer to every man that asketh you a reason of the hope that is in you with meekness and fear." [1 Peter 3:15 KJV].

We are now in a quite different battleground. We are now fighting the real enemy of humanity. I was done fighting against flesh and blood as I served our flag and country. We are now fighting the prince of principalities, and we will not let the flag of our Christian faith to touch the ground for God, in His name, and for His glory.

Ephesians 6:10-20 "10 Finally, my brethren, be strong in the Lord, and in the power of his might. 11 Put on the whole armour of God, that ye may be able to stand against the wiles of the devil. 12 For we wrestle not against flesh and blood, but against principalities, against powers, against the rulers of the darkness of this world, against spiritual wickedness in high places. 13 Wherefore take unto you the whole armour of God, that ye may be able to withstand in the evil day, and having done all, to stand. 14 Stand therefore, having your loins girt about with truth, and having on the breastplate of righteousness; 15 And your feet shod with the preparation of the gospel of peace; 16 Above all, taking the shield of faith, wherewith ye shall be able to quench all the fiery darts of the wicked. 17 And take the helmet of salvation, and the sword of the Spirit, which is the word of God: 18 Praying always with all prayer and supplication in the Spirit, and watching thereunto with all perseverance and supplication for all saints; 19 And for me, that utterance may be given unto me, that I may open my mouth boldly, to make known the mystery of the gospel, 20 For which I am an ambassador in bonds: that therein I may speak boldly, as I ought to speak." [Ephesians 6:10-20 KJV]

The battlefield is no longer on the ground. It is way up beyond what we can see in the skies. It is with Satan and with his angels. It is against the darkness of this world. When we obeyed God, I knew the devil would not be happy because I am about to start my new life in the ministry. It was not something the devil would be pleased with. I could picture the scene in heaven in my mind when Job was in his full potential and obedience to God. Satan went up to God and started accusing Job until God gave him the permission to touch Job. I inserted the whole chapter one from the book of Job for your convenience, and for you to meditate on.

Job 1:1-22 "1 There was a man in the land of Uz, whose name was Job; and that man was perfect and upright, and one that feared God, and eschewed evil. 2 And there were born unto him seven sons and three daughters. 3 His substance also was seven thousand sheep, and three thousand camels, and five hundred yoke of oxen, and five hundred she asses, and a very great household; so that this man was the greatest of all the men of the east. 4 And his sons went and feasted in their houses, everyone his day; and sent and called for their three sisters to eat and to drink with them. 5 And it was so, when the days of their feasting were gone about, that Job sent and sanctified them, and rose up early in the morning, and offered burnt offerings according to the number of them all: for Job said, It may be that my sons have sinned, and cursed God in their hearts. Thus did Job continually. 6 Now there was a day when the sons of God came to present themselves before the Lord, and Satan came also among them. 7 And the Lord said unto Satan, Whence comest thou? Then Satan answered the Lord, and said, From going to and fro in the earth, and from walking up and down in it. 8 And the Lord said unto Satan, Hast thou considered my servant Job, that there is none like him in the earth, a perfect and an upright man, one that feareth God, and escheweth evil? 9 Then Satan answered the Lord, and said, Doth Job fear God for nought? 10 Hast not thou made an hedge about him, and about his house, and about all that he hath on every side? thou hast blessed the work of his hands, and his substance is increased in the land. 11 But put forth thine hand now, and touch all that he hath, and he will curse thee to thy face. 12 And the Lord said unto Satan, Behold, all that he hath is in thy power; only upon himself put not forth thine hand. So Satan went forth from the presence of the Lord. 13 And there was a day when his sons and his daughters were eating and drinking wine in their eldest brother's house: 14 And there came a messenger unto Job, and said, The oxen were plowing, and the asses feeding beside them: 15 And the Sabeans fell upon them, and took them away; yea, they have slain the servants with the edge of the sword; and I only am escaped alone to tell thee. 16 While he was yet speaking, there came also another, and said, The fire of God is fallen from heaven, and hath burned up the sheep, and the servants, and consumed them; and I only am escaped alone to tell thee. 17 While he was yet speaking, there came also another, and said, The Chaldeans made out three bands, and fell upon the camels, and have carried them away, yea, and slain the servants with the edge of the sword; and I only am escaped alone to tell thee. 18 While he was yet speaking, there came also another, and said, Thy sons and thy daughters were eating and drinking wine in their eldest brother's house: 19 And, behold, there came a great wind from the wilderness, and smote the four corners of the house, and it fell upon the young men, and they are dead; and I only am escaped alone to tell thee. 20 Then Job arose, and rent his mantle, and shaved his head, and fell down upon the ground, and worshipped, 21 And said, Naked came I out of my mother's womb, and naked shall I return thither: the Lord gave, and the Lord hath taken away; blessed be the name of the Lord. 22 In all this Job sinned not, nor charged God foolishly." [Job 1:1-22 KJV]

I do not claim to be perfect like Job. The reason why I shared the first chapter of Job is because of the trials and sufferings that came to us when we started stepping in the will of God. When we obey God with all our hearts and whole being, we can expect the devil to try to interfere, hinder, and perhaps even destroy us. It may mean sailing in the midst of the storm and waves of physical illness. It may mean financial hardships. The devil may touch our family or marital relationship. In my case, the Lord allowed a thorn in the flesh to be part of my life to humble me and keep me close to Him.

As a military retiree, I really got busy. I worked during the day and went to Bible Institute at night to further my knowledge. It was a great privilege for me to be in the service for our country, but I am more privileged to be in the service of God. We had our own share of hardships, but God's grace is sufficient, and His mercy is new every morning. There is nothing permanent in this old world but God's mercy and faithfulness. The Bible says in Lamentations 3:22-25 "22 It is of the Lord's mercies that we are not consumed, because his compassions fail not. 23 They are new every morning: great is thy faithfulness. 24 The Lord is my portion, saith my soul; therefore, will I hope in him. 25 The Lord is good unto them that wait for him, to the soul that seeketh him." [Lamentations 3:22-25 KJV]

There was no turning back for us. In obedience to God's calling in our lives we have joined the battle for lost souls. In Paul's letter to Timothy, he encourages believers to fight the good fight of faith. We are privileged to be in the service of the King of kings and Lord of lords.

TRAGEDY EVEN
IN OBEDIENCE

I have suffered from back pain since my Army days. The demands of being a soldier really took a toll on me. I had continually sought treatment for it through the years. What started out as a routine treatment ended in the loss of my ability to walk.

I am greatly confident, and it is my personal belief that God made us stewards of the good and of the difficult things that happen in our lives. I say this because my experience of pain and suffering was God's way of shaping me. I had to guard my heart from bitterness and allow God to make me the way He wanted me to be. He is the potter, and I am the clay. I must yield to Him and find peace, even during the painful refining process. I was about to graduate from Bible Institute when the Lord allowed me to have a life altering experience. The good Lord allowed a thorn in my flesh. He let me go through this to not only make me grow and mature, but also to make me feel what others feel when they go through hard times as they touch the ground of suffering and pain. One thing was sure, I believe God was preparing me for His perfect plan.

The medical procedure which went wrong and paralyzed me from the waist down was part of God's plan. God allowed it to happen. I would not be here right now sharing my testimony if I did not go through this experience. God had brought me to a point in my life where only He could help. I can certainly relate to what the Bible says in Psalm 147:3 "He healeth the broken in heart, and bindeth up their wounds" [Psalm 9:3 KJV], and in Romans 8:28 "And we know that all things work together for good to them that love God, to them who are the called according to his purpose" [Romans 8:28 KJV]. I was in a place in my life where I had no strength left and God was my only hope. What I learned was that if all I had left is God, then I have everything!

I walked into the clinic where the procedure was going to be performed that winter morning. I left the clinic in a gurney and was transported to the Emergency Room (ER) of a nearby hospital. From the ER, I ended up in a room which would be my home for the next 51 days. All I could do was stare at the ceiling as I became more aware that I could not move any part of my body from the waist down. I also had no trunk control at all. The nurses helped me to sit up, but I would fall in all directions. My wife and children were all looking at me with so much love but so much sorrow. I knew that they, like me, could not comprehend what happened to me. They were there for me, but I still felt alone, trapped in my body which could no longer do what I wanted it to do. The fear and anxiety as I faced an uncertain future, were overwhelming.

I had a team of medical professionals help me navigate my new physical condition: a hospitalist, a rehabilitation doctor, a neurologist, an occupational therapist, a physical therapist, and the ever so helpful nurses. Yet, none of them could tell what kind of recovery I would have, if any. All I knew was that if I were to get better, the healing would come from the hand of God. God could have healed me instantly like the lame man in the Bethesda pool in John chapter 5, but that was not His plan.

He gave me this thorn in the flesh so He can use me in my weakness. That was what He did to Apostle Paul in 2 Corinthians 12:7-10 "7 And lest I should be exalted above measure through the abundance of the revelations, there was given to me a thorn in the flesh, the messenger of Satan to buffet me, lest I should be exalted above measure. 8 For this thing I besought the Lord thrice, that it might depart from me. 9 And he said unto me, My grace is sufficient for thee: for my strength is made perfect in weakness. Most gladly therefore will I rather glory in my infirmities, that the power of Christ may rest upon me. 10 Therefore I take pleasure in infirmities, in reproaches, in necessities, in persecutions, in distresses for Christ's sake: for when I am weak, then am I strong." [2 Corinthians 12:7-10 KJV]

PARALYSIS

I spent my first day in the hospital in a deep state of shock. The following days did not get any easier as the realization that my paralysis and the resulting complications might be permanent. My body was unable to do the simplest tasks. Turning in bed, bending my knees, or just moving my toes was in the realm of the impossible. I had to wear a compression device on my legs so that I would not develop blood clots. I always had to wear foot braces so that I would not develop footdrop. Due to indwelling catheters, I developed urinary tract infections often. The steroids I had to take to reduce the inflammation in my spinal cord caused my sugar to shoot up. My arms hurt and my shoulders were swollen as I learned to slide my body while seated so I could move from the bed to the wheelchair and from the wheelchair to the commode. My legs were nothing but dead weight. I even had to be tied to the commode so I would not fall over. It took assistance from the nurses and my wife for me to be able to do things that I used to take for granted. Also, I had a long list of medications that I had to take. The hardest part was adjusting to the fact that my brain and my body were no longer in sync. My mind was as active as before, but my body would not and could not do its most basic functions. The days in the hospital went by slowly as pain and grief kept me close company. The once strong soldier was now paralyzed, and the hope of recovery was dim. How I wished the Lord would heal me instantaneously as He did to the man sick of palsy in Mark 2:1-12.

Mark 2:1-12 "[1] And again he entered into Capernaum after some days; and it was noised that he was in the house. [2] And straightway many were gathered together, insomuch that there was no room to receive them, no, not so much as about the door: and he preached the word unto them. [3] And they come unto him, bringing one sick of the palsy, which was borne of four. [4] And when they could not come nigh unto him for the press, they uncovered the roof where he was: and when they had broken it up, they let down the bed wherein the sick of the palsy lay. [5] When Jesus saw their faith, he said unto the sick of the palsy, Son, thy sins be forgiven thee. [6] But there were certain of the scribes sitting there, and reasoning in their hearts, [7] Why doth this man thus speak blasphemies? who can forgive sins but God only? [8] And immediately when Jesus perceived in his spirit that they so reasoned within themselves, he said unto them, Why reason ye these things in your hearts? [9] Whether is it easier to say to the sick of the palsy, Thy sins be forgiven thee; or to say, Arise, and take up thy bed, and walk? [10] But that ye may know that the Son of man hath power on earth to forgive sins, (he saith to the sick of the palsy,) [11] I say unto thee, Arise, and take up thy bed, and go thy way into thine house. [12] And immediately he arose, took up the bed, and went forth before them all; insomuch that they were all amazed, and glorified God, saying, We never saw it on this fashion." [Mark 2:1-12 KJV]

I was told by the doctors that I may never walk again. I could not wrap my mind around that possibility. I was deeply grieved that I might have to face the future as a paraplegic. I also shed tears for the loss of the life I once knew. Yet, in my darkest moments, I found strength and hope in God's Word. In Joshua 1:9, the Bible says "Have not I commanded thee? Be strong and of a good courage; be not afraid, neither be thou dismayed: for the LORD thy God is with thee whithersoever thou goest." [Joshua 1:9 KJV] This verse was a great encouragement to me.

SIX DAYS

Number six is man's number. I love number seven. But unfortunately, it was not the number they gave me in my journey of faith and my battle with physical difficulties. I was a soldier for twenty-four years. From my basic training days to my retirement, I did not get wounded nor did I get even a scratch. But the number six made an impact in my life. This six-day war for me in my hospital bed was overwhelming. My battlefield this time was in my mind and in my heart. There was a battle between what I know my God could do and the bleak prognosis from my doctors. There was a battle between hope and despair.

What is with the 'Six Days' anyways? My doctor who had worked with problems like mine for 45 years gave me the not so pleasant news. I was told that after six days if I still could not move any part of my body from the waist down, I would be paralyzed for life.

The days after that were a big blur. In the beginning, the challenges I had to face just to make it through each day kept my mind off the dread of the future. As the days went by, the gravity of my physical condition started to weigh heavily in my heart. There were days when I could not pray because of exhaustion, both physical and emotional. That said, I will always be grateful for the prayers spoken on my behalf. I will forever be grateful for a merciful God who heard those prayers and carried me through the hardest of times.

STRENGTH IN WEAKNESS

Six days came and went and there was no significant change in my condition. I found it difficult to accept what the doctors told me my life would be. I hung on to what I knew in my heart my God could do. Days turned into weeks and my days were spent in physical and occupational therapy and waiting for my doctors to come visit, always hoping that they would somehow bear any kind of good news. Little victories like the time when I was able to move my right big toe and when I started being able to wiggle my feet were celebrated and brought happy tears to me and my family. Occasionally, a patient on a walker passed by in the hallway. I would tell myself that if only I could do that, I would be really grateful. Being in a wheelchair and having another person decide which way and where to go had its way of teaching me humility and gratitude. Long days in my hospital bed taught me patience with my body which started recovering, if ever so slowly. I thought I learned life's biggest lessons while I was in the Army. The training that I went through at boot camp, the discipline I learned in the military, and all the hardships that I endured during my twenty four year military service, helped shape who I am.

Little did I know that I would learn life's other important lessons in my hospital bed.

My seemingly hopeless state also taught me to keep seeking God's face and keep my faith in my ever-merciful God for He was and is my only hope. I begged God for healing, and I prayed like never before. Pouring out my heart to God every day somehow gave me some peace. I wished God would ask me what He did to the lame man at the pool in Bethesda and heal me like He healed him.

Here is the story of what happened at the pool with the helpless and sick man in John 5:1-15 "1 After this there was a feast of the Jews; and Jesus went up to Jerusalem. 2 Now there is at Jerusalem by the sheep market a pool, which is called in the Hebrew tongue Bethesda, having five porches. 3 In these lay a great multitude of impotent folk, of blind, halt, withered, waiting for the moving of the water. 4 For an angel went down at a certain season into the pool, and troubled the water: whosoever then first after the troubling of the water stepped in was made whole of whatsoever disease he had. 5 And a certain man was there, which had an infirmity thirty and eight years. 6 When Jesus saw him lie, and knew that he had been now a long time in that case, he saith unto him, Wilt thou be made whole? 7 The impotent man answered him, Sir, I have no man, when the water is troubled, to put me into the pool: but while I am coming, another steppeth down before me. 8 Jesus saith unto him, Rise, take up thy bed, and walk. 9 And immediately the man was made whole, and took up his bed, and walked: and on the same day was the sabbath. 10 The Jews therefore said unto him that was cured, It is the sabbath day: it is not lawful for thee to carry thy bed. 11 He answered them, He that made me whole, the same said unto me, Take up thy bed, and walk. 12 Then asked they him, What man is that which said unto thee, Take up thy bed, and walk? 13 And he that was healed wist not who it was: for Jesus had conveyed himself away, a multitude being in that place. 14 Afterward Jesus findeth him in the temple, and said unto him, Behold, thou art made whole: sin no more, lest a worse thing come unto thee. 15 The man departed, and told the Jews that it was Jesus, which had made him whole." [John 5:1-15 KJV]

God had other plans for me and a different purpose for what He allowed in my life. 2 Corinthians 1:3-4 says "3 Blessed be God, even the Father of our Lord Jesus Christ, the Father of mercies, and the God of all comfort; 4 Who comforteth us in all our tribulation, that we may be able to comfort them which are in any trouble, by the comfort wherewith we ourselves are comforted of God." [2 Corinthians 1:3-4 KJV]. My recovery was slow and would be incomplete. Through it all, He was and is my comfort. I was comforted so I would be a comfort to others and bear good news of God's loving kindness.

UNDERSTANDING
MY INJURY

The spinal cord is the body's information highway that the brain uses to send and receive signals to the different body parts. Motor signals from the brain tell our muscles what to do while sensory signals from the different parts of the body tell our brain whether we are hot or cold, or whether there is pressure or pain. Spinal cord injury means that this highway is somehow compromised. All the muscles and nerves below the level of the injury may be affected. More damage may occur over days or weeks because of inflammation in and around the spinal cord. Hence, not all complications will be immediately apparent.

In my case, my injury meant that the motor signals that my brain was sending to the lower parts of my body could not get through because the highway or message carrier was severely damaged, resulting in paralysis. I also suffered from neuropathic pain in both feet. I had a constant burning sensation that felt like my feet were on top of hot coals. It was because my brain was receiving signals from a damaged spinal cord. My brain then interpreted it as pain even though there was no actual injury to my feet.

My doctors could treat the symptoms but could not really do anything to make me heal. Even physical therapy could only strengthen the muscles the corresponding nerves of which were not damaged or were healing from the injury. As days passed, I learned that my injury had other lifelong implications.

51 DAYS

I was admitted to the hospital on January 21, 2011 and was confined for treatment and rehabilitation for a total of fifty-one days. That was long and dreadful, not just for me, but also for my loved ones. Remember the doctor said that in six days if I was not be able to move my legs, I would be bed ridden for life? It was based on his experience as a rehabilitation doctor. He had treated patients with varying spinal cord injuries, so he had a strong understanding of my situation. I was extremely sad, and my family felt the same way. I think it was just natural to go through a grieving process after a life-changing injury. After forty days, I saw hope when I began to see some improvements in the movement of my lower extremities. I began to do twice as many repetitions of the required exercises. My family's presence, support, and devotion for me were a big encouragement. Without them, I do not know how I could have dealt with what happened to me. It really helped how I emotionally dealt with my situation. Although my wife did not show it to me at the hospital, but when I felt better and had recovered some of my strength, she mentioned to me that she went through deep sorrow too. Her dad was dying from cancer at that time. She was heartbroken and was grieving for what was happening to both her dad and me. She also said that she felt like she lost her sense of security as she could no longer lean on me as her protector. On the rare occasions when she would go home from the hospital, she would cry and pour out her heart to the Lord. She would go and pray in her closet so that our children would not hear her sobbing. I am sure our children had a hard time dealing with the situation as well. I made sure I still talked to them about their plans, their future, their studies, and their dreams. I asked them to cling to God for He was our only hope.

One of the most unforgettable times that I had in the hospital was when my pastor and fellow church members celebrated my birthday with my family in the dining room. I really appreciated their presence, the uplifting songs they sang, their gifts of love, and the time they spent with me. I felt so special. It was an encouragement to me. When I was stuck in my hospital bed, every minute spent with family and friends was precious. The simple birthday celebration was a big deal because of all the love they had shown me. I felt the embrace of God in those precious moments.

It was during those times when God gave me the assurance that He would be with me and everything would be alright. It may have looked like it was my greatest nightmare, but in the midst of it all, I felt He was with me. I had the assurance from His Word that everything would work together for my good. While it was true that I could not control my body, I knew that everything was under His control. Healing was beyond my doctor's reach, but there was nothing my God could not do.

I was in my final semester in the Bible Institute. Regardless of my state, I was determined to complete my theological studies. With the help of my pastor I started taking classes again. He brought the materials and audio recordings of the courses to the hospital so that I could finish my studies and graduate on time with my classmates. Sometimes, we even held class sessions in my hospital room. Even after my release from the hospital, I was not physically able to attend classes at our church and my pastor continued to bring me the materials at home.

I remember every day vividly. My daughter Catherine, who was doing her student nursing at the same hospital, would stop by and say hello. I know she tried to look brave and did her best to cheer me up. It was her last semester of nursing school so I told her that it would be best if she concentrated on her studies. My son Allen had to stop going to school because my wife needed a hand on the many occasions when I had to be lifted and carried. He was there every day and assisted me anyway he could. After my release from the hospital, he along with my wife were the ones who took me to the many physical therapy sessions and my various doctors' appointments. He had to drive long distances for my appointments in Los Angeles. He would push my wheelchair and sometimes had to carry me because I was unable to support my own body. He also assisted my wife with my personal care. I am grateful I had my family by my side when I needed them the most.

My siblings drove long hours to visit me whenever they could. My wife and I practically lived in the hospital. She never left my side except for brief moments she had to go home to shower or to get a change of clothes.

BASIC TRAINING AGAIN

My fifty-one days at the hospital were like Basic Training again for me. My occupational therapist had to teach me how to do a lot of things without the use of my legs. I had to learn simple tasks like putting on my socks and shoes, changing my clothes, and even washing my face while on a wheelchair. Everything that was not within my reach had to be handed to me. I also had to be taught exercises to relieve the pain as the ligaments in my shoulders had become inflamed. I had to use my shoulders a whole lot to carry the weight of my body so I could slide from one point to another. I felt like a helpless little child who could not manage without the aid of an adult.

Physical therapy was also a regular part of my schedule. I was strapped to a tilting table and the table was turned vertically so my legs could carry the weight of my body. I was also given a lot of exercises to strengthen my leg muscles. I was advised that these exercises should be a regular part of my regimen otherwise muscle atrophy would set in. I lost a lot of muscle mass because of the paralysis. I remember a particular day when I ended up sobbing in the therapy room. A psychiatrist was asked to see me the following day. I was advised by the psychiatrist that my grief was a normal emotional reaction to what happened to me. She never came by again after that.

A highlight of my rehabilitation was a field trip to my favorite restaurant. As we got there, we had to get handicap parking that would allow space for the wheelchair and look for a ramp that would lead me to the dining area. A place so familiar to me now seemed foreign as I became more aware of the changes in my life. That was the first time I left the hospital and ventured out in the outside world as a person with disability.

As months passed, God blessed, and I started to slowly regain some movement. These blessings gave me hope that walking, even with the aid of a walker or a cane, would someday be possible.

Four months after my injury, my dad passed away in the Philippines. All my siblings went home. Due to my condition, I was not able to attend his funeral. It broke my heart, but God reminded me of the day I shared the gospel to my parents. Both accepted Jesus Christ as their Savior. This comforted me that my dad was now with the Lord in heaven. As what the Bible says in 2 Corinthians 5:8 "We are confident, I say, and willing rather to be absent from the body, and to be present with the Lord." [2 Corinthians 5:8 KJV]

IN THE POTTER'S HAND

It was God's amazing grace that sustained me in my fifty-one day stay at the hospital. He did not leave me nor forsake me. The Bible says in Hebrews 13:5, "5 Let your conversation be without covetousness; and be content with such things as ye have: for he hath said, I will never leave thee, nor forsake thee" [Hebrews 13:5 KJV]. God's promise gave me hope. In the confines of my hospital room, I felt His presence and sweet embrace. In the midst of the storm, I have never felt closer to God. Every time I read His Word; I was always assured that He would take care of me. My worries about ever walking again, the future of my family, and going to the mission field were not for me to figure out. One of the verses that spoke to my heart and helped me to be still, surrender, and find peace in God's hands, is found in Isaiah 64:8 "But now, O LORD, thou art our father; we are the clay, and thou our potter; and we all are the work of thy hand" [Isaiah 64:8 KJV]. I am but clay and He is my Maker and my God. My healing was not immediate. It took a while before I could stand on my own and carry my own weight. I was in a wheelchair for a year and a half. In fact, I was in my wheelchair when I finally received my Theological Studies diploma. For that, I am grateful. After two years of physical therapy I was finally able to walk with a walker and a little later, with a rollator. While the doctors thought that I may never walk again, God knows best. I was not supposed to be able to drive again but God made it that my right leg is a little stronger than my left. God has been really good to me. Praise the Lord!

I believe with all my heart that what I went through was meant to be a refining process. God wanted me to be strong in my faith and He wanted me to be an instrument of His grace. My paralysis taught me lessons I probably would not have learned otherwise. I loved God before the incident, but my helplessness taught me to cling and to trust Him more, and to really wait on His timing. It was He who allowed me to lose my ability to walk for a season. He allowed it so I would get to know Him more. He allowed it because He wanted to work on me and shape me to become the person He wanted me to be. God allowed it so that I could share my experience and tell others about God's power and goodness.

Now, I can bring the gospel of hope to the lost and dying world. I can share my story of healing and God's miracle in my life. Now I know helplessness and hopelessness, but I also have seen God's healing power. Now I can boldly talk about my loving and faithful God. Because of my experience, I can talk to people about marriage and what true love and commitment are. Now, I can talk to people about loyalty and how my wife's faithfulness and support helped me to keep going during the darkest days in my life. Now, I know that all is in the Potter's hands and He has a plan for each of us so He can accomplish His purpose. We are here to yield to the Potter's hands so we can be who and what He wants us to be. Now, I know more than ever that God is sovereign, and He can take a useless lump of clay like me to make a useful vessel. And finally, I know that the clay can never understand the mind of the Potter unless it yields to His hands and finds peace in His will.

MISSION FIELD

After two years of rehabilitation, my legs were still weak, but I was able to walk better with the aid of a rollator. I was ordained and sent off to the Philippine mission field. The Philippines was a challenge for a person like me because of the lack of provision for handicap access. Though it was hard, I still had to execute the mission I was given by God as a soldier of the cross. My life's course has been severely altered due to my injury, but it never occurred to me to just quit. As I have learned from the Army, a wounded soldier could still fight. I knew that with every step I would take, God was and is with me.

We visited many churches, preached the Word, helped, and partnered with many pastors all over the country. We worked alongside them as they do work for the Lord. Our desire is to be an encouragement to the Christian soldiers on the frontline. We want to be what Barnabas was to Paul, a friend, and a fellow worker to God's soldiers. We took part in pastors and workers' conferences, medical missions, and youth meetings. We drove to the far north, went to the central provinces, and even reached Mindanao in the southern Philippines where the biggest Muslim population in the country lives. We helped start and support many children's feeding programs. These ministries provided opportunities for children in impoverished neighborhoods to hear the gospel of salvation. After they are taught lessons from the Bible, they are fed.

As we tread the path that God gave us, I always share my testimony of how God made me walk again. I am a living testimony that God really fulfills His promise. God uses my trial to show the world that He was and still is in the healing and saving business today. I give God all the glory for everything He has done. My prayer is for the Lord to give me and my wife good health as we continue to serve Him.

A NEW STORM

Since 2013, we spend most of the year in the Philippines and only come back to the US for my annual medical checkups and to spend precious time with our children. In 2017, an unexpected visitor just sneaked in and caught me by surprise. It was something that would accompany me wherever I went and whatever I did. I suffered from severe back pain every day. On the scale level of 1 to 10, it was an eight at its worst. One early morning, I could hardly walk to go to the bathroom. My back pain was debilitating. It reminds me of what the Bible says in 2 Corinthians 12:5-10 "5 Of such an one will I glory: yet of myself I will not glory, but in mine infirmities. 6 For though I would desire to glory, I shall not be a fool; for I will say the truth: but now I forbear, lest any man should think of me above that which he seeth me to be, or that he heareth of me. 7 And lest I should be exalted above measure through the abundance of the revelations, there was given to me a thorn in the flesh, the messenger of Satan to buffet me, lest I should be exalted above measure. 8 For this thing I besought the Lord thrice, that it might depart from me. 9 And he said unto me, My grace is sufficient for thee: for my strength is made perfect in weakness. Most gladly therefore will I rather glory in my infirmities, that the power of Christ may rest upon me. 10 Therefore I take pleasure in infirmities, in reproaches, in necessities, in persecutions, in distresses for Christ's sake: for when I am weak, then am I strong." [2 Corinthians 12:5-10 KJV]. It was a difficult time for me, but I knew that God's grace would be sufficient, and His strength is made perfect in my weakness.

Because of the severe pain, we were not able to travel and visit churches. We saw a neurologist and they did an X-Ray and an MRI. It was revealed that the severe pain was caused by bulging discs that needed to be decompressed. We were advised that the decompression procedure must be done immediately to prevent permanent damage to my nerves. We were hesitant to have the procedure done in the Philippines. The surgeon there was planning to put steel rods and screws on my back. We were informed by a sister in-law about the neurosurgeon that she knew in Singapore, and we were introduced to him.

We went to Singapore to see the specialist. Traveling by land and air with the pain I had was an awful experience. After the initial visit, he immediately performed a discoplasty procedure to release the pressure from my bulging discs. By the grace of God, the procedure gave me the desired relief. I was able to walk with a lot less pain. We were advised that what he did was just to release the pressure and that a bone fusion was necessary to prevent the pain from reoccurring. The neurosurgeon in Singapore referred us to his friend in Cedars Sinai Hospital in California. Within a couple of weeks, we were back in California for the fusion surgery. The doctor performed two levels of decompression and transforaminal lumbar interbody fusions. Surgical hardware was applied to my spine to help enhance the fusion rate and to provide stability in the area. Screws and rods were attached to the back of my vertebra and spacers were inserted into the L4-L5 and L5-S1 disc spaces of my spine. A bone graft was placed into the space and alongside the back of the vertebra to be fused. As the bone graft healed, it fused my vertebra above and below and formed one long bone. You could call me bionic man now, but I cannot wait to put on the spiritual body someday.

GOD IS WITH ME

They made me sign a contract for decompression and transforaminal lumbar interbody fusion surgery. The risks were numerous, among them getting paralyzed again and even dying from the procedure.

There were about 4 to 6 doctors that worked on me during the surgery. They had a computer that could tell the surgeon if he was about to hit a nerve. I felt at ease because of the advanced technology and the good doctors that I had; but more so, because I know God was and is in control. He is our great Healer and Physician. He knew what He was doing in my life. I was encouraged because our pastor and assistant pastor from our home church, Faith Baptist Church Canoga Park, were there and prayed for me before the procedure. My wife and children were there. I was in surgery for more than 7 hours. When I woke up in the recovery room, the first thing I did was to thank the Lord and worship Him for what He has done. Thankfully, the surgery on my back eliminated the excruciating pain that bothered me for a long time. Before the surgery, the pain was unbearable. Now, the pain is significantly decreased. Praise God! To God Be the Glory!

THE MISSION CONTINUES

In Mark 16:15, God commanded His followers with this verse "15 And he said unto them, Go ye into all the world, and preach the gospel to every creature." [Mark 16:15 KJV]

After my last surgery and rehabilitation, we were back in the mission field in 2018. Our local partners in the ministry were excited and encouraged to see us. Again, we continued where we left off; visiting churches, preaching, and helping with many feeding programs for hungry children and at the same time preach the gospel to them. We see those children as living souls. After meeting their urgent physical need, we proceed to meet their spiritual need which is of outmost importance. Along with many partner churches, we preach the salvation gospel to them. The strategy works well; they are more attentive when their stomach is full. The enemy is also busy trying to feed these children's minds with the wrong gospel. Truly, the devil is going around looking whom he may devour. Regardless of how much hardships we go through as missionaries, it is well worth it. Just to have the opportunity to preach the gospel to them, plant, and water the seed in children's hearts, is enough to fill our hearts with so much joy. This is enough incentive to any missionary.

One day while meeting with some local pastors, they mentioned that they have been praying for a bible institute to be started locally. I inquired at a church in California if we could use their bible institute's curriculum. By the grace of God, they were thrilled to let us use their entire four-year curriculum. God put everything in place for us. Hence, the Lighthouse Bible Institute Philippines was born. More than thirty students are currently attending. Before, the long commute to Manila and the cost of travel had discouraged many from taking bible classes.

These experiences in the mission field are a testament that when we are in line with God's will, good things happen. We pray that our Lord will continue to give us physical and spiritual strength and continue to use us in the Philippines.

MY TESTIMONY

I was born and raised in the Philippines. Growing up, my parents rarely went to church. I was taught to be a good person. I could only hope that somehow my good deeds would outweigh my sins so that when I die my soul would go to heaven. I never heard the true salvation gospel preached when I was in our village.

My family and I immigrated to the United States in the 1980s. We were a family of rice farmers in the Philippines. We left the small farming village and came to the US, the land of milk and honey. More importantly, our departure paved the way for me to hear the Gospel. I am extremely grateful that the Lord brought us here.

I fulfilled my dream of joining the US military by enlisting in the US Army in 1983. I thought of myself as extremely fortunate and a blessed man. For the first time in my life, I had a stable job and my own money. I thought life was great then. A few years after that, I married my dear beautiful wife Cecile. We were later blessed with a daughter, Catherine and a son, Allen. We were stationed in various military bases in the US, Europe, and Asia. I enjoyed all of them especially Germany and Japan, but I remember Hawaii the most because it was where the most significant event of my life happened. I heard the Gospel for the very first time and got saved. I accepted the Lord Jesus Christ as my Lord and Savior. I have since realized that it is not my good works that would bring my soul to heaven but what Jesus did on the cross for me. Salvation is not something that I could earn for myself but is a free gift from God. It was a great blessing that God saved me, in spite of the kind of person I was. It is all about grace indeed. My wife and I were saved the same day. We were baptized a few months after that.

After we got saved, we started serving the Lord in the children's ministry. I later joined the choir and then eventually, we were out witnessing. We tried to be faithful in serving our Lord everywhere we went. When we got stationed in Japan, God called me to be a missionary evangelist to the Philippines. I felt humbled because God chose me to be His servant. At the same time, I was scared and felt inadequate. I thought of the verses in 2 Timothy 2:3-4 when God said "Thou therefore endure hardness, as a good soldier of Jesus Christ. No man that warreth entangleth himself with the affairs of this life; that he may please him who hath chosen him to be a soldier" [2 Timothy 2:3-4 KJV]. I told myself I must please God who has chosen me to be a soldier of Jesus Christ. I certainly believe in what C.T. Studd once wrote "Only one life, 'twill soon be past, only what's done for Christ will last."

I retired from the United States Army in 2007. I learned from the military that we should never go to war unprepared. With all the training I received serving under several pastors, I still felt ill-equipped to go to the mission field. Hence, I enrolled in a bible institute in California. In 2011, five months before I graduated, I sought treatment for my back pain. Something went wrong with the procedure and it left me paralyzed from the waist down. I was bedridden and wheelchair bound for more than a year. I could not comprehend what happened to me. I could not even move my toes. I did not know if I would ever walk again and if I would still be able to go to the mission field. Through it all, my wife stayed by my side and took care of me. Then one day God comforted me. I felt His presence and assurance. God put it in my heart that I would walk again. It took more than two years but as God promised, I was able to walk again with a rollator. I am grateful for everything God has done in my life!

Since 2013, my wife and I have been in the Philippine mission field working and partnering with many pastors. We want to be an encouragement to the soldiers in the battlefield. Our part is to plant and water the seed. It is God who gives the increase. 1Corinthians 3:6 "I have planted, Apollos watered; but God gave the increase" [1Corinthians 3:6 KJV] 6]. We are beyond grateful for God's goodness and faithfulness in our lives.

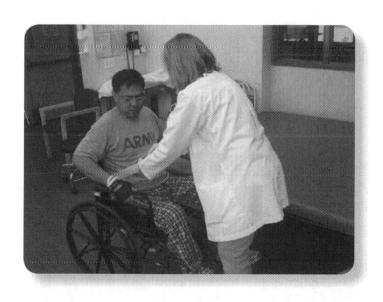

ABOUT THE AUTHOR

Catalino Carino was born in San Quintin, Pangasinan, Philippines. He is married to the former Cecilia Maclang Cruz of Malolos, Bulacan, Philippines. He was blessed by the Lord with two children Catherine and Allen who love the Lord.

Mr. Carino joined the United States Army in October of 1983. He was stationed in various military bases in the US, Asia, and Europe. He was promoted to the rank of Master/First Sergeant. After 24 years of military service, he retired in July 2017. He earned many military awards and decorations to include Defense Meritorious Service Medal (2nd Award), Meritorious Service Medal (2nd Award), Army Commendation Medal (2nd Award), Army Achievement Medal (6th Award), Joint Meritorious Unit Award (2nd Award), Army Superior Unit Award, Army Good Conduct Medal (7th Award), National Defense Service Medal (2nd Award), and Global War on Terrorism Service Medal to name a few.

He graduated from Park University, Parkville, Missouri with a bachelor's degree in Computer Science. He finished his Theology Studies at Fundamental Baptist Bible Institute, Ventura, California. He is also studying bachelor's in Business Management with Laurus College, Oxnard, California.

Please check his Web page and follow him on Social Media.

https://www.facebook.com/Journey-of-a-US-Army-Soldier-to-Gods-Army-106993461197425

ACKNOWLEDGEMENT

Praise God for His goodness in my life!

Writing a book was tougher than I ever imagined and more rewarding than I could have ever envision. None of this would have been possible without my wife, Cecile. She devoted much time to work with me and helped me tell my story. She was as vital to this book getting done as I was. Thank you so much, Honey.

I thank the Lord that my path crossed with Pastor Ely Sagansay's when we were in the mission field in the Philippines. He heard about how God worked in my life and encouraged me to share my life story.

Printed in the United States
By Bookmasters